# THE POWER OF PREVAILING FAITH

*"...for as a prince hast thou power with God and with men, and hast prevailed."*

**Genesis 32:28**

by

Franklin N. Abazie

***The Power of Prevailing Faith***
COPYRIGHT 2017 BY Franklin N Abazie
ISBN: 978-1-945133-49-7

Published by:  F N ABAZIE PUBLISHING HOUSE- aka, Empowerment Bookstore.

*That I may publish with the voice of thanksgiving and tell of all thy wondrous works.*
**Psalms 26:7**

To order additional copies, wholesales
or booking:
Call the Church office (973-372-7518),
or Empowerment Bookstore Hotline (973-393-8518)

Worship address:
343 Sanford Avenue Newark New Jersey 07106
Administrative Head Office address:
33 Schley Street Newark New Jersey 07112
Email:pastorfranknto@yahoo.com
Website www.fnabaziehealingministries.org
Publishing House:  www.fnabaziepublishinghouse.org

This book is a production of F N Abazie Publishing House. A publication Arms of Miracle of God Ministries 2017. First Edition

# CONTENTS

# THE MANDATE OF
# THE COMMISSION

"The moment is due to impact your world through the revival of the healing & miracle ministry of Jesus Christ of Nazareth."

"I am sending you to restore health unto thee and I will heal thee of thy wounds, said the Lord of Host."

# ARMS OF THE COMMISSION

1) F N Abazie Ministries-Miracle of God Ministries (Miracle Chapel Intl)

2) F N Abazie TV Ministries: Global Television Ministry Outreach

3) F N Abazie Radio Ministries: Radio Broadcasting Outreach

4) F N Abazie Publishing House: Book Publication

5) F N Abazie Bible School: also called Word of Healing Bible School (W.O.H.B.S)

6) F N Abazie Evangelistic Ass: Miracle of God Ministries: Global Crusade

7) Empowerment Bookstore: Book distribution

8) F N Abazie Helping Hands: Meeting the help of the needy world wide

9) F N Abazie Disaster Recovery Mission: Global Disaster Recovery

10) F N Abazie Prison Ministry: Prison Ministry for all convicts "Second chance"

**Some of our ministry arms are waiting the appointed time to commence.**

# INTRODUCTION

I may never get the chance to meet you in person. For the most part, my titles are the books I will love to read. From the title of this book, *"The Power of Prevailing Faith."* There is a level of faith that prevails against any obstacle in life. It is that power of prevailing faith that I will be sharing in this publication.

In my own opinion, unless we all develop *prevailing faith in life*, we will never succeed in any area of our choice of pursuit. This book titled *the power of prevailing faith is a book written out of faith in God* for the purpose of motivating and encouraging every reader that as long as we endure in faith we shall prevail with answers.

*"We travail in prayers to prevail with answer in life"*—Franklin N Abazie

Among the several reasons that I have written this book is to strengthen the believer concerning their individual prayer life. Until Jacob travail in prayers, he was not guaranteed to prevail with a change of name. *"And he said, Thy name shall be called no more Jacob, but Israel: for as a prince hast thou power with God and with men, and hast prevailed."* **Genesis 32:28**

This publication will encourage you to keep believing and trusting in God. We have tried to share a bit of what the Holy Spirit is saying about the *Power of prevailing faith*. This small book brings clarity over some prevailing contradiction concerning *prevailing power of faith*.

It is my personal desire to see this little book make sense in your life. It will please our Heavenly Father *if you will repent today of all your sins. We must develop a relationship with our Lord Jesus Christ.* Hell is certain, Heaven is real! *I admonish you in the Lord, you must make a plan to make heaven at last (eternity). May the Holy Spirit guide and lead you the remaining days of your life.*

Happy Reading!

*"And the hand of the children of Israel*

*prospered, and prevailed*

*against Jabin the king of Canaan,*

*until they had destroyed*

*Jabin king of Canaan."*

*Judges 4:24*


*"Thus the children of Israel were*

*brought under at that time,*

*and the children of Judah prevailed,*

*because they relied upon the*

*LORD God of their fathers."*

*2 Chr 13:18*

"And Asa cried unto the LORD his God, and said, LORD, it is nothing with thee to help, whether with many, or with them that have no power: help us, O LORD our God; for we rest on thee, and in thy name we go against this multitude. O LORD, thou art our God; let not man prevail against thee."

2 Chr 14:11

*So David prevailed over the Philistine*

*with a sling and with a stone, and*

*smote the Philistine, and slew him;*

*but there was no sword in the*

*hand of David.*

*1 Sam 17:50*

HIS DESTINY WAS THE
**CROSS....**

HIS PURPOSE WAS
**LOVE.....**

HIS REASON WAS
**YOU....**

# ENGAGING THE POWER OF FAITH

We must *first believe in God for faith in* Him, to work for our lives. We must be action oriented because *faith is action* oriented in my opinion. Nothing changes in life until we take action in life. If we claim to have faith, then we must be action ready to move into the supernatural. We must always trust and have confidence in God and in ourselves. Nobody is our God, therefore never trust on anybody in life.

For Anyone to prevail in faith we must first develop a will power. Queen Esther said, *"if I perish, I perish."* Unless we are determined to fight to finish, it is not prevailing faith.

We must always *believe in God* and in our own abilities to get things accomplish in life. We must first discover ourselves before others discover the talents in us. We must recognize our strength and weakness before we make certain decisions in life. You are certain to get the worst of the bargain when you exchange ideas with the wrong person. In this race of life, always make friends with those who can inspire you, those you can learn from. The bible says He that walketh with wise men shall be wise: but a companion of fools shall be destroyed.

Try to always be able to differentiate those God planted into your life for a season and for a long term. Information and continual learning is the key to succeed in life. Always choose your friends wisely, for an evil companion can corrupt good manners. Remember, "he that walk with the wise shall be wise." In the time of prosperity we recognize our friends. *"Wealth maketh many friends."* **Proverb 19:4** But in the time of adversity our friends know us, *"and there is a friend that sticketh closer than a brother."* **Proverb 18:24**

Always recognize those who make you a special person in their lives. Never make people significant in your life when you are only an option to them. The less you associate with some people the more your life will improve. Remember Abraham did not become rich until he separated from lot his nephew. "And the Lord said unto Abram, after that Lot was separated from him, Lift up now thine eyes, and look from the place where thou art northward, and southward, and eastward, and westward: For all the land which thou seest, to thee will I give it, and to thy seed forever." **Genesis 13:14-15**

Anytime time you allow mediocrity in others, it increases your mediocrity. An important attribute in successful people is their impatience with failure, negative thinking, and mediocrity. As we grow in life, our association will eventually change over time.

Eventually, you will disconnect from those that failed to improve their lives and you will connect and make friends with other successful people going up higher in the race of life. Never receive counsel from unproductive negative thinking people, never discus your trial and challenges with those incapable of contributing to the solution or solving your problems. Always look for the best in people around you. Develop a forgiving heart, a thankful countenance, and praiseful spirit.

Always remember this, if you are going to achieve excellence in big things, you must develop the habit in little matters. Collin Powell once said and I quote "A dream doesn't become a reality through magic, it takes sweat, determination, and hard work." There is no secret to success, it is the result of preparation, hard work, and learning from failure." Excellence is not an exception, it is a prevailing attitude.

We must develop the habit of confronting all prevailing challenges facing our lives. Remember there is always away OUT for you, there is also away UP for you and away FORWARD for us all in life as long as we believe in God and have faith.

# PREVAILING FAITH
# INSPIRATION

1) Always remember that your present situation is not your final destination. The best is yet to come.

2) Sometimes the bad things that happen in our lives put us directly on the path of the best things that will ever happen to us.

3) If you don't like where you are, move. You are not
a tree.

4) You can't start the next chapter if you keep reading the last.

5) If it doesn't open, it's not your door. Watch it!

6) Sometimes you need to stop outside, get some air, and remind yourself of who you are and where you want to be.

7) Sometimes you need to talk to a three year old, just so you can understand life again.

8) Listen & silent are spelled with the same letters. Think about it.

9) Sometimes, you have to stop thinking so much and just go where your heart takes you.

10) You don't have to have it all figured out to move forward.

11) Never stop believing because miracles happen
every day.

# HOW TO PREVAIL IN FAITH AND IN LIFE

## ~The Power of a Mental Picture

God said to Jeremiah, what seeeth thou?

Moreover the word of the Lord came unto me, saying, Jeremiah, what seest thou? And I said, I see a rod of an almond tree. Then said the Lord unto me, Thou hast well seen: for I will hasten my word to perform it. **Jer 1:11-12** *If I am permitted to say it this way. "We must capture the picture of our future through the scriptures."*

*"If you can see ahead, know ahead, you will go ahead in life."* Mental pictures are so important because they show you, the actual future ahead. It takes *prevailing faith in God* to believe in a future you cannot see right now.

The Lord also said to Abraham.

And the Lord said unto Abraham, after that Lot was separated from him, Lift up now thine eyes, and look from the place where thou art northward, and southward, and eastward, and westward: For all the land which thou seest, to thee will I give it, and to thy seed forever. **Genesis 13:14-15**

Every time God speaks in faith, we must *believe in God*. Speaking of Abraham, the bible says *"Who against hope believed in hope, that he might become the father of many nations, according to that which was spoken, So shall thy seed be."* **Romans 4:18** Abraham became the father of many nations once he believed God.

## ~The Power of Positive Mindset

It takes a positive, and overcomer's mindset to overcome opposition, fear, and the mockers of our destiny. Unless we develop a positive mindset we will never make an impact in our generation. *"And Caleb stilled the people before Moses, and said, Let us go up at once, and possess it; for we are well able to overcome it."* **Number 13:30**

If we must prevail in life we must develop a positive mindset in life. I see you prevailing against all odd, and challenges opposing you in life.

It is written *"And the Lord said, Behold, the people is one, and they have all one language; and this they begin to do: and now nothing will be restrained from them, which they have imagined to do."* **Genesis 11:6**

If we must prevail in faith and in life, we must develop a positive mindset against every prevailing obstacle of life.

# CHAPTER 1

## PREVAILING FAITH

*"And Jesus answering saith unto them, Have faith in God."*
**Mark 11:22**

Unless we develop *prevailing faith in God* we will never make an impact in life. Faith in God is all it takes for maximum impact in life. *It is written for whatsoever is born of God overcometh the world: and this is the victory that overcometh the world, even our faith. Who is he that overcometh the world, but he that believeth that Jesus is the Son of God?* **1 John 5:4-5**

*How do I develop prevailing faith against sickness?*

**"And he said unto him, Arise, go thy way: thy faith hath made thee whole." Luke 17:19**

One great man once said and I quote, *"Just because you are not sick right now does not mean you are healthy."* For most people every time we talk about healing, they rush and conclude that it has to deal with sickness. Well,

1

may I tell you the truth? Healing by definition comprises of a lot of things, depending how you define it. If you are broke (poor in life) for example, then your finances need the healing for you to prosper. If you are unemployed you need the healing power to gain employment. If you are sick on your body, then you need the healing balm of Gilead- from the master physician Jesus to heal you. In my own opinion, healing is medicinal, physical, financial marital e.t.c.

Although healing is physical as well as spiritual, it takes faith in God, for healing to take place. This I mean, we must believe in the validity of the power of God to heal. Sin and sickness came as a result of Adams and Eve disobedience. Jesus brought us healing and salvation- meaning deliverance from sin and sickness.

As Christians we are not supposed to be sick. In the redemptive blessing includes salvation from sin and sickness, or healing from sin and sickness. The Greek word *sozo* means *saved and made whole*. It is my prayer that if you are sick in any part of your body that you will be healed even as you read this book in Jesus Mighty Name.

**"But without faith it is impossible to please him: for he that cometh to God must believe that he is, and that he is a rewarder of them that diligently seek him." Hebrew 11:6**

The power of prevailing faith will not heal, deliver, or save anyone unless we have faith and believe in our heart. Just like the above scripture says, "but without faith it is impossible to please him." Faith is the plat form for healing and deliverance. *"And he Jesus said unto her, Daughter, be of good comfort: thy faith hath made thee whole; go in peace."* Luke 8:48

There some prevailing sickness that require only the power of prevailing faith to overcome it in life. To the contrary, the medical community have accepted faith healing as a way to cure some outstanding incurable diseases. I encourage you, whatever may be the prevailed sickness, and deliverance, have faith in God and you shall overcome it in Jesus Name. *"For whatsoever is born of God overcometh the world: and this is the victory that overcometh the world, even our faith."* 1 John 5:4

**"Jesus saith unto him, Thomas, because thou hast seen me, thou hast believed: blessed are they that have not seen, and yet have believed." John 20:29**

For the most part, we focus exclusively on faith healing mystery, forgetting that we must "BELIEVE IN GOD." Faith in God is the primary tool for healing. Scriptures proved that Jesus couldn't do any mighty work, because he marveled at their unbelief. " And he could there do no mighty work, save that he laid his hands

3

upon a few sick folk, and healed them. And he marveled because of their unbelief. And he went round about the villages, teaching. (Mark 6:5-6) Unbelief in God, is a stumbling hindrance that will hinder the flow of healing into our lives. It takes our faith in God to initiate our desired healing from God.

Although our *faith in God* initiates our desired healing, the mystery of healing depend solely on God-the Mighty physician. It is inevitable for the Almighty to withhold our healing in time of need, because healing is his children bread. Remember Healing is the will of God. It is written "Beloved, I wish above all things that thou mayest prosper and be in health, even as thy soul prospereth." (3 John 1:2)

Our faith in God, moves Him to save us. "For by grace are ye saved through faith; and that not of yourselves: it is the gift of God:" (Ephesians 2:8) Salvation means deliverance from sins and destruction of the devil. Inside of salvation includes our healing- which is the will of God. "That it might be fulfilled which was spoken by Isaiah the prophet, saying: He Himself took our infirmities and bore our sicknesses" (Matt. 8:17; Is. 53:4-6)

# HINDERANCES TO THE HEALING FAITH

## ----*Doubt*----

We are instructed by the Holy scripture that *"...let the weak say, I am strong."* (Joel 3:10) As long as we doubt in our heart healing cannot take place in our life, It is written *"A double minded man is unstable in all his ways."* (James 1:8)

Every time we are in doubt, we hinder the stretched arm of the Lord to heal us. If we must be healed from sickness and diseases we must cast out all doubt and fear in the mighty name of Jesus.

## ----*Unbelief*----

Every time we don't believe in life, we make the word of God ineffective in our life. Often we misunderstand how God operates. Listen, God is spirit and we must believe spiritual things for anything supernatural to be activated in our lives. It is written, "And he could there do no mighty work, save that he laid his hands upon a few sick folk, and healed them. And he marveled because of their unbelief. And he went round about the villages, teaching." (Mark 6:5-6) Unbelief is one of the strong

5

hindrance to healing that it can even affect the faith healer.

## ----*Fear*----

A lot of people are afraid in life for nothing. They just panic and dramatize any little challenge in life. I pray we cast out all such spirits. We are told "There were they in great fear, where no fear was: for God hath scattered the bones of him that encampeth against thee: thou hast put them to shame, because God hath despised them." (Psalms 53:5) It is written, "For God hath not given us the spirit of fear; but of power, and of love, and of a sound mind." (2 Timothy 1:8) God heals us with our faith, while the devil tortures and attacks us with sickness by instilling fear in our heart. "There is no fear in love; but perfect love casteth out fear: because fear hath torment. He that feareth is not made perfect in love." (1 John 4:18)

Remember........

"For ye have not received the spirit of bondage again to fear; but ye have received the Spirit of adoption, whereby we cry, Abba, Father" (Romans 8:15)

## ----*Dishonors the faith healer*----

It is written, "Be it far from me; for them that honour me I will honour, and they that despise me shall be lightly esteemed." (1 Samuel 2:30) We must honor God's agents of healing- the prophet.

"Therefore whoever confesses Me before men, him I will also confess before My Father who is in heaven. But whoever denies Me before men, him I will also deny before My Father who is in heaven." (Matt 10:32-33) For God to pay attention concerning our desired healing, we must honor His prophets sent our way. Most God's prophets who are also faith healers carries the mantle of healing concerning our lives. We must question and key into it if we must experience God dynamics healing mystery.

Healing is a mystery of the works of faith in God. But faith cannot work unless there is love in place. It is written but faith which worketh by love. (Gal 5:6)

Remember........

"And we have known and believed the love that God hath to us. God is love; and he that dwelleth in love dwelleth in God, and God in him." (1 John 4:16)

We must prove our love for God by

our service to others and to His kingdom. We must accept the free gift of salvation for the redemption of our soul. We must embrace spirituality if we must make an impact and prosper in our lifetime.

"What is the mystery of faith"?

"And this is the confidence that we have in him, that, if we ask any thing according to his will, he heareth us:" (1 John 5:14)

"Who against hope believed in hope, that he might become the father of many nations, according to that which was spoken, So shall thy seed be.And being not weak in faith, he considered not his own body now dead, when he was about an hundred years old, neither yet the deadness of Sarah's womb: He staggered not at the promise of God through unbelief; but was strong in faith, giving glory to God; And being fully persuaded that, what he had promised, he was able also to perform." (Romans 4:18-22)

## WE MUST REPENT OUR SINS

Wherefore seeing we also are compassed about with so great a cloud of witnesses, let us lay aside every weight, and the sin which doth so easily beset us, and let us run with patience the race that is set before us. (Hebrew 12:1)

We must not allow sin to destroy our calling and destiny in life. We must therefore repent of any known sin in our lives before God can restore our destiny.

**For sin shall not have dominion over you: for ye are not under the law, but under grace. Romans 6:14**

Every time we yield to sin, we place ourselves in captivity. We must all strive to forsake sin and do away with every evil that dent our Christian dignity. Know ye not, that to whom ye yield yourselves servants to obey, his servants ye are to whom ye obey; whether of sin unto death, or of obedience unto righteousness? (Romans 6:16)

It is written, Be not overcome of evil, but overcome evil with good. (Romans 12:21) We must all repent of any know sin that dents our Christian walk with the Lord Jesus Christ.

Apostle Paul had this to say....

I find then a law, that, when I would do good, evil is present with me. For I delight in the law of God after the inward man: But I see another law in my members, warring against the law of my mind, and bringing me into captivity to the law of sin which is in my members. O wretched man that I am! who shall deliver me from the body of this death? I thank God through Jesus Christ our Lord. So then with the mind I myself serve the law of God; but with the flesh the law of sin. (Romans 7:21-25)

The above scripture makes a lot of sin if you examine your own life. Evil is present every time we strive to do good. What shall we say then? Shall we continue in sin, that grace may abound? God forbid. How shall we, that are dead to sin, live any longer therein? **Romans 6:1-2**

*"Examine yourselves, whether ye be in the faith; prove your own selves. Know ye not your own selves, how that Jesus Christ is in you, except ye be reprobates?"* **2 Cor 13:5**

Although most faith people live in denial about the work of the flesh, from my own scriptural understanding everyone operating within the scope of Galatians 5:20-21 is classified as a sinner.

# HOW DO I COME OUT OF SIN?

Although we are all sinners, it takes a will power of the mind for us to repent and come out of sin. So many people have died because they could not repent of the sin that easily beset them. Drug addicts who turned pastors have died because they went back into their old addiction. A great man of God who repented because of alcohol in the family died of excessive alcohol abuse. We must make up our mind for good if we must come out of sin. We must confess, and forsake it in the mighty name of Jesus.

The word says as many as received him, to them gave He power to become the sons of God. Even to them that believe on his name.

To qualify for divine visitation, do the following with sincerity—

1) Acknowledge that you are a sinner and that He died for you. (Romans 3:23)

2) Repent of your sins. (Acts 3:19, Luke 13:5, 2 Peter 3:9)

3) Believe in your heart that Jesus died for your sin. (Romans 10:10)

4) Confess Jesus as the Lord over your life. (Romans 10:10, Acts 2:21)

### Now repeat this Prayer after me

*Say Lord Jesus, I accept you today, as my Lord and my savior, forgive me of my sins wash me with your blood. Right now, I believe, I am sanctified, I am save, I am free, I am free from the Power of sin to serve the Lord Jesus. Thank you Lord for saving me. Amen.*

Congratulations: You are now...

A BORN AGAIN CHRISTIAN.

### Again I say to you—

### CONGRATULATIONS!

# CHAPTER 2

## THE FIGHT OF FAITH

*"Fight the good fight of faith, lay hold on eternal life, whereunto thou art also called, and hast professed a good profession before many witnesses."*
**1 Timothy 6:12**

As long as I am concerned, faith is a fight. Every day we exercise our faith on just the smallest decision and action we take. Life is full of risk, therefore as believers of Jesus Christ, we must overcome every opposition and the obstacles that come our way. The bible encouraged us to be strong and courageous. I am persuaded to tell you even as you read the pages of this book, you shall overcome every challenge and trial facing your life in Jesus Mighty Name.

For unless we understand that we are in a warfare, the enemy will keep assaulting, and attacking our lives. We must put up the good fight of faith.

## What does it mean to fight the good fight of faith?

On a daily basis, our faith in God is challenged and harassed by fear, doubt, lack of money or job, etc. The good fight of faith literally means to keep on believing in God regardless of the trials, irrespective of the shortcoming, we should never fall into doubt and unbelieve in life. Most of us think, we do not have faith. Often we discourage ourselves. we let fear grip our mind. As Christians, we all have faith to a great degree. It is written, *"For I say, through the grace given unto me, to every man that is among you, not to think of himself more highly than he ought to think; but to think soberly, according as God hath dealt to every man the measure of faith."* **Romans 12:3**

To fight the good fight of faith means to endure to the end as soldiers of Jesus Christ. Everyone must make up their mind especially in this tough times that we live in.Jesus said it clearly in John chapter sixteen verse thirty-three *"These things I have spoken unto you, that in me ye might have peace. In the world ye shall have tribulation: but be of good cheer; I have overcome the world."* **John 16:33**

Whenever trials and trouble face us in life, we must remain in faith and in charge. We must not let fear, and doubt to overpower our faith. It's easy for us to feel like we've got great faith when things go well for us. *"We operate in faith all the time and don't even think about it."*

I'm not talking about big decision making or life changing moves but the little things here and there , that we do not pay attention to. we must exercise our faith in God to confront any obstacle of life.

*We all have faith, but we must put it to use. One great man, I respect dearly in my whole life is president Abraham Lincoln. He was a man of tested faith. How many of us will go through what he went through in life and still succeed? Below is the life story of the obstacles and challenges faced by Abraham Lincoln in his lifetime.*

## Abraham Lincoln fought the good fight of faith in his lifetime

Probably the greatest example of the fight of faith is the life of Abraham Lincoln. He was born into poverty, Lincoln was faced with defeat throughout his life. He lost eight elections, twice failed in business, and suffered a nervous breakdown. But he never gave up on his pursuit in life. Abraham Lincoln fought the good fight of faith to the finish.

He could have quitted several times, but he refused to give up the victory to the devil. Because he didn't quit, he became one of

the greatest presidents in the history of USA.
Lincoln was a champion and he never gave up.

*Below is the fight of faith that led him into the
white house in 1860.*

**1816:** His family was forced out of their
home. He had to work to support them.

**1818:** His mother died.

**1831:** Failed in business.

**1832:** Ran for state legislature – lost.

**1832:** Also lost his job – wanted to go to law
school but couldn't get in.

**1833:** Borrowed some money from a friend to
begin a business and by the end of the year
he was bankrupt. He spent the next 17 years
of his life paying off this debt.

**1834:** Ran for state legislature again – won.

**1835:** Was engaged to be married, sweetheart
died and his heart was broken.

**1836:** Had a total nervous breakdown and
was in bed for six months.

**1838:** Sought to become speaker of the state legislature – defeated.

**1840:** Sought to become elector – defeated.

**1843:** Ran for Congress – lost.

**1846:** Ran for Congress again – this time he won – went to Washington and did a good job.

**1848:** Ran for re-election to Congress – lost.

**1849:** Sought the job of land officer in his home state – rejected.

**1854:** Ran for Senate of the United States – lost.

**1856:** Sought the Vice-Presidential nomination at his party's national convention – got less than 100 votes.

**1858:** Ran for U.S. Senate again – again he lost.

**1860:** Elected president of the United States.

Although there are so many biblical
characters like David, Joseph, and Daniel who
also fought the fight of faith. This noble mentor
Abraham Lincoln, whom I admire dearly is a
noted example whom we can emulate in life.
*"My mother used to say health comes before
wealth." As long as there is life we must keep
up the fight of faith. I see you succeeding in
the midst of challenges in Jesus Mighty Name.
Amen.*


# HINDERANCES TO THE FIGHT
# OF FAITH

## ~*Pride*

*"The bible says that pride goeth before
destruction. "Pride goeth before destruction,
and an haughty spirit before a fall."* **Proverb
16:18**

Often must folks will quit in a heartbeat.
*The fight of Faith* is not a cheap talk. It is easy
to confess in faith than to put faith into action
in life. The spirit of pride will deter and hinder
anyone from putting up the fight of faith.
Although Abraham lincoln suffered several
losses in life, he was still determined to fight
to the finish. Despite all Joseph struggles in

the bible, joseph was still determined to not only survive in Egypt but to become the prime minister of the land of Egypt.

## ~Low self-esteem

In my opinion, most believers settle for less in life due to lack of self-esteem. Everyone must develop the spirit of the fight of faith if we must prevail against our daily trials and tribulation of life.For unless you think great, do what attracts greatness in life, you will never become great in life.

## ~Poor man's mentality

It is written, *"Now there was found in it a poor wise man, and he by his wisdom delivered the city; yet no man remembered that same poor man.*
*Then said I, Wisdom is better than strength: nevertheless, the poor man's wisdom is despised, and his words are not heard."* **Ecll 9:15-16**
Abraham Lincoln was born into poverty, but he became the president of the USA. We are told by the Holy scripture that, as a man thinks in his heart, so is he. Poor mentality will hinder anyone from putting up the fight of faith against every challenge of life. For unless you think big, and rich, you will never experience it in life.

# ACCESS INTO THE SUPERNATURAL

## BE BORN AGAIN:

We must be born again for us to experience the supernatural and mentorship. **John 3:3-8**

**Jesus answered and said unto him, Verily, verily, I say unto thee, Except a man be born again, he cannot see the kingdom of God. Nicodemus saith unto him, How can a man be born when he is old? can he enter the second time into his mother's womb, and be born? Jesus answered, Verily, verily, I say unto thee, Except a man be born of water and of the Spirit, he cannot enter into the kingdom of God.**

**That which is born of the flesh is flesh; and that which is born of the Spirit is spirit. Marvel not that I said unto thee, Ye must be born again. The wind bloweth where it listeth, and thou hearest the sound thereof, but canst not tell whence it cometh, and whither it goeth: so is every one that is born of the Spirit.**

We must therefore obey the voice of the Lord, confess him as Lord and savior then we can learn from his teaching and position our lives to encounter the supernatural.

## THE FEAR OF GOD:

One of the greatest channels to position our lives to encounter the supernatural is to covet the spirit of the fear of God. The fear of the Lord is the beginning of wisdom: and the knowledge of the holy is understanding. (Proverb 9:10)

## RIGHTEOUS LIFESTYLE:

It may take a longer time, but over the cause of your lifetime it will show. Righteousness is a virtue that tells everybody around you, the way you live, the way you do business and the way you operate. "For the vision is yet for an appointed time, but at the end it shall speak, and not lie: though it tarry, wait for it; because it will surely come, it will not tarry." (Hab 2:3)

## INTEGRITY

**The integrity of the upright shall guide them:.......Proverb 11:3**

As long as you carry integrity in your heart, it will guide your life from all assaults and attacks of the devil. So he fed them according to the integrity of his heart; and guided them by the skillfulness of his hands. (Psalm78:72)

# AGREEMENT

Until you agree with the Holy Spirit by believe God's word to be true, you will forever suffer frustration. Once you agree with the Holy Spirit, you are guaranteed access into the supernatural. Again I say unto you, That if two of you shall agree on earth as touching any thing that they shall ask, it shall be done for them of my Father which is in heaven. (Matthew 18:19)

For where two or three are gathered together in my name, there am I in the midst of them. Mathew 18:20. Remember.... The Lord thy God in the midst of thee is mighty. (Zeph 3:17)

# SOUL WINNING

It is written.... **and he that winneth souls is wise. Proverb 11:30** Soul winning is the gate way into the supernatural. As long as you win souls for Jesus he will decorate your life and destiny.

# CONCLUSION

"Go, gather together all the Jews that are present in Shushan, and fast ye for me, and neither eat nor drink three days, night or day: I also and my maidens will fast likewise; and so will I go in unto the king, which is not according to the law: and if I perish, I perish." **Esther 4:16**

I challenge you today to make up your mind, develop a will power, and confront all obstacles facing you in life. *"What you fail to confront, you cannot conquer."*

We must all come unto repentance if we must encounter our savior Jesus Christ. Repentance is the key to deliverance, protection, and promotion. Everyone that desired to encounter testimonies in their prayer must confess and forsake their sinful ways and go after God. **Eccl1 2:13-14**

Let us hear the conclusion of the whole matter: Fear God, and keep his commandments: for this is the whole duty of man.

For God shall bring every work into judgment, with every secret thing, whether it be good, or whether it be evil.

The entire book will remain a story to everyone who is not ready to make a decision for Jesus Christ. One man said if you failed to plan we have planned to fail in life. We want you to make plans to make heaven. The bible says in Eccl: 12:14. For God shall bring every work into judgment, with every secret thing, whether it be good, or whether it be evil. If you are a born again Christian; we like to encourage you in your Christian life. If you are not a born again Christian we can help you here receive genuine salvation.

## HAVE YOU DISCOVERED YOUR GIFT FROM GOD?

A man's gift maketh room for him, and bringeth him before great men. (Proverb 18:16)

Although God wants you to breakthrough in life, you have a greater role to play in this covenant relationship. Remember Joseph's gift in the bible brought him before the King. Daniel gift in the bible brought him before four presidents and kings.

Discover your talent from God and pursue it with all your might. You must recover your destiny in the Mighty Name of Jesus. Do not give up in life concerning your destiny because winners do not quit. Never waste any day of your life because your time is your money.

# FAVOR CONFESSION

*Father thank you for making me righteous and accepted through the blood of Jesus Christ. Because of that, I am blessed and highly favored by God. I am the subject of your affection. Your favor surrounds me as a shield, and the first thing that people see around me is your favored shield.*

*Thank you that I have favor with you and man today. All day long people go out of their way to bless me and help me. I have favor with everyone that I deal with today. Doors that were once closed are now opened for me. I receive preferential treatment, and I have special privileges, I am Gods favored child.*

*No good thing will he withhold from me. Because of Gods favor my enemies cannot triumph over my life. I have supernatural increase and promotion. I declare restoration to everything that the devil has stolen from my life. I have honor in the midst of my adversaries and an increase in assets, especially in real estate and expansion of territories.*

*Because I am highly favored by God, I experience great victories, supernatural turnarounds, and miraculous breakthrough in the midst of great impossibilities. I receive recognition, prominence, and honor. Petitions are granted to me even by ungodly authorities. Policies, rules, regulations, and laws are changed and reverse on my behalf.*

*I win battles that I don't even have to fight, because God fights them for me. This is the day, the set time and the designated moment for me to experience the free favor of God, that profusely and lavishly abound on my behalf in Jesus name. Amen.*

# YOU MUST BE BORN AGAIN

If you are a born again Christian; we like to encourage you in your Christian life. If you are not a born again Christian we can help you here receive genuine salvation. (2 Cor 5:17) **Therefore if any man be in Christ, he is a new creature: old things are passed away; behold, all things are become new.**

**Now repeat this Prayer after me**

*Say Lord Jesus, I accept you today, as my Lord and my savior, forgive me of my sins wash me with your blood. Right now, I believe, I am sanctified, I am save, I am free, I am free from the Power of sin to serve the Lord Jesus. Thank you Lord for saving me. Amen.*

Congratulations: You are now...

A BORN AGAIN CHRISTIAN.

**Again I say to you—**

**CONGRATULATIONS!**

### *What must I do to determine my divine visitation?*

To determine divine visitation you must be born again! The word says, *"As many as received him, to them gave He power to become the sons of God. Even to them that believe on his name."* (John 1:12)

To qualify for divine visitation, do the following with sincerity—

1) Acknowledge that you are a sinner and that He died for you. (Romans 3:23)

2) Repent of your sins. (Acts 3:19, Luke 13:5, 2 Peter 3:9)

3) Believe in your heart that Jesus died for your sin. (Romans 10:10)

4) Confess Jesus as the Lord over your life. (Romans 10:10, Acts 2:21)

### Now repeat this Prayer after me

*Say Lord Jesus, I accept you today, as my Lord and my savior, forgive me of my sins wash me with your blood. Right now, I believe, I am sanctified, I am save, I am free, I am free from the Power of sin to serve the Lord Jesus. Thank you Lord for saving me. Amen.*

Congratulations: You are now...

A BORN AGAIN CHRISTIAN.

### Again I say to you—

### CONGRATULATIONS!

**I adjure you to watch the Spirit of God bear witness with your Spirit confirming His word with signs following. The word says The Spirit itself beareth witness with our spirit, that we are the children of God.** Join a bible believing church or join us on our weekly and Sunday worship services at 343 Sanford Avenue Newark New Jersey 07106.

# WISDOM KEYS

— Every Productive Society is a society heading to the top.

— Millions of Nigerians run away from Nigeria, very few Nigerians stay in Nigeria.

— My decision to return Nigeria is the will of God for my life.

— My short coming in America after 18 years, trained me to be wise, to think, reflect and reason appropriately.

— If you train your mind to reason it will train your hands to earn money.

— It is absurd to use the money of the heathen to build the kingdom of the living God.

— Every Ministry reveals its agenda and goal either at the beginning or at the end. Be careful of your life it is your first Ministry.

— The average American mind is conditioned for a continual quest to get new things and (discard the former) and throw away old things.

— When I considered well, my BMW jeep became my initial deposit for the work of the ministry in Nigeria.

— Money will never fall from any tree.

— Everyone is waiting for you to change your mind until you change your thinking nothing changes around you.

— Multiple academic degrees in other discipline gave me the chance to think, reflect and reason.

— What so everyone are thinking and reflecting at the moment reveals you to the time and the now factor .

— All events and intents are the product of precise thought processes, accurate reason every event is designed for a designated timeline.

— Wisdom is your ability to think, to create and invent. If you can think wise enough you will come out of penury.

— The distance between you and success is your creative ability to think reason and reflect accurate.

— Success is the result of hard work, commitment resolve and determination learning from past mistakes and failing.

— If you organize your mind you have organized your life and destiny.

— There is a thin line between success and failure. If you look above and beyond you are on your way to success.

— Wealth is your ability to think, power is your ability to reason and success is your ability to be informed.

— If you can make use of your mind by thinking and reasoning God will make use of your life and destiny.

— Think and Be Great.

— Reflect, Reason, Think and Be Great.

— Famous people are born of woman.

— That you will make it is your intention; that you will survive is your resolve, that you will succeed with changes is your determination, personal efforts and hard work.

— No man was born a failure. Lack of vision is the end product of failure.

— Working with mental patients encourages and aspire me to be a productive observant and dedicated to my assignment.

— Successful people are not magicians, it is the will power combined with hard work, and determination and a resolve to succeed that make them succeed.

— In the unequivocal state of the mind, intention is not a location or a position it is the state of the mind.

— So many people think, that they think. The mind is used to think, reflect, and reason. You will remain blind with your eye open until you can see with your mind by thinking.

— There is no favoritism in accurate and precise calculation.

— Although knowledge is power, information is the key and gateway to a great future.

— It will take the hand of God to move the hand of man.

— With the backing of the great wise God, nothing will disconnect you from your inheritance.

— As long as you have wisdom and understanding of God, Satan and evil cannot manipulate your life and destiny.

— You have come this far by yourself judgment and decision you have made in the past, now lean and listen to God for another dimension of greatness.

— Great people are common people it is extra ordinary effort and the price of sacrifice that produces greatness.

— As a mental direct care worker I saw a great pastor and a motivational speaker within myself.

— Menial job does not reduce your self-worth, until you resolve to achieve greatness see greatness in all you do; you will never count in your community.

— The principle of Jesus will solve your gambling and addiction problems.

— The man of Jesus will lead you into heaven,

— Everyone have their self-appraisal and what they think about you. Until you discover yourself other opinion about you will alter the real you.

— Supervisors and directors are just a position in the chain of command in a work place. Never allow your supervisor hierarchy to alter your opinion about yourself.

— Everyone can come out of debt if they make up their mind.

— That I am not a decision maker at work does not diminish my contribution to my world.

— Although it appears like it was a poor decision to accept a direct care employment at a psychiatric hospital as I reflect of my nine years of experience, it became apparent that I have learnt and experienced enough for my next assignment in life.

— Self-encouragement and determination is a resolve of the heart.

— If you are determined to make a difference, and do the things that make a difference you will eventually make a difference.

— Good things do not come easy.

— Short cuts will cut your life short.

— Those who look ahead move ahead.

— Life is all about making an impact. In your life time strive to make an impact in your community.

— Make friends and connect with people who are moving ahead of you in life.

— If you can look around well you have come a long way in your life, made a lot of difference and realized a lot of success in life.

— If you are my old friend, hurry up to reach out to me before I become a stranger to you.

— Everything I am blessed with inspirations from God, that change my definition and interpretation of the world around me.

— I thought I was stagnant and lonely until I looked around and noticed my children running around and my wife cooking.

— At 40 I resigned my Job to seek the Lord forever.

— My ministry took a drastic rise to the top when the wisdom of God visited me with knowledge and understanding.

— You will be a better person, if you understand the characteristics of your personality – your mood swings, attitudes, and habits.

— It is the seed of love you sow into the heart of a child and a woman that you reap in due time.

— Love is not selfish, love share everything including the concealed secrets of the mind.

— As long as you have a prayer life and a bible; you will never feel lonely, rejected, and idle in the race of life.

— When good friends disconnect from you, let them go, they might have seen something new in a different direction.

— Confidence in yourself and in God is the only way to bring you out of captivity.

— Never train a child to waste his/her time.

— The mind is the greatest assets of a great future.

— You walk by common sense run by principles and fly by instruction.

— Those who fly in flight of life fly alone.

— Up in the air you are alone. No one can toll you accept the compass of knowledge and information.

— I have seen a towing vehicle I have seen a towing ship I have never seen a tolling airplane.

— I exercise my judgment and make a decision every minute of the day.

— Decisions are crucial, critical and vital with reference to your future.

— So many people wish for a great future. You can only work towards a great future.

— Your celebrity status began when you discovered your talent. What are you good at? Work at it with all commitment.

— Prayers will sustain you but the wisdom of God will prosper you.

— When I met Oyedepo, his teachings changed my perspective. But when I met Ibiyeomie; His teaching changed my perception.

— I will be successful in ministry if only I concentrate and focus my energy in the work of the ministry.

— It took the late Dr. Vincent Pearle Norman's book to open my mind towards kingdom success.

# CHAPTER 3

## PRAYER OF SALVATION

It will profit us nothing as a ministry if after reading this book, your salvation is still questionable. I long to see you saved and delivered from all the wiles and schemes of the devil.

### ARE YOU SAVED?

The honest truth is that the Lord Jesus really does not know you unless you are saved. For as many as are led by the Spirit of God, they are the sons of God. For ye have not received the spirit of bondage again to fear; but ye have received the Spirit of adoption, whereby we cry, Abba, Father. The Spirit itself beareth witness with our spirit, that we are the children of God:Romans8:14-16

### *What must I do to determine my divine visitation?*

To determine divine visitation you must be born again! The word says as many as received him, to them gave He power to become

40

the sons of God. Even to them that believe on his name.

To qualify for divine visitation, do the following with sincerity—

1) Acknowledge that you are a sinner and that He died for you. (Romans 3:23)

2) Repent of your sins. (Acts 3:19, Luke 13:5, 2 Peter 3:9)

3) Believe in your heart that Jesus died for your sin. (Romans 10:10)

4) Confess Jesus as the Lord over your life. (Romans 10:10, Acts 2:21)

### Now repeat this Prayer after me

*Say Lord Jesus, I accept you today, as my Lord and my savior, forgive me of my sins wash me with your blood. Right now, I believe, I am sanctified, I am save, I am free, I am free from the Power of sin to serve the Lord Jesus. Thank you Lord for saving me. Amen.*

Congratulations: You are now...

A BORN AGAIN CHRISTIAN.

**Again I say to you—**

**CONGRATULATIONS!**

I adjure you to watch the Spirit of God bear witness with your Spirit confirming His word with signs following. The word says The Spirit itself beareth witness with our spirit, that we are the children of God.

# MIRACLE CARE OUTREACH

*"...But that the members should have
the same care one for another"*
**1 Corinthians 12:25**

We are all members of the body of Christ. Jesus commanded us to love our neighbor as ourselves. This includes caring for one another as a member of one body. True love is expressed in caring and giving. The word says for God so Love He gave....

Reach out to someone in need of Jesus, help someone in crisis find Christ. Look out and prove your love to Jesus by caring and inviting your friends and associates to find Jesus the Healer.

Invite your friends to our Home Care Cell Fellowship (Miracle chapel Intl Satellite fellowship) In the USA at 33 Schley Street Newark New Jersey 07112. Home Care Cell fellowship Group meets every Tuesday at 6:00pm-7:00pm.

If you are in Nigeria—**MIRACLE OF GOD MINISTRIES**, aka "**MIRACLE CHAPEL INTL**" Mpama –Egbu-Owerri Imo state Nigeria.

# LIFE IS NOT ALL ABOUT DURATION— BUT ITS ALL ABOUT DONATION

What does the above statement mean?....

Life consists not in accumulation of material wealth. (Luke 12:15) But it's all about liberality...i.e., what you can give and share with others. (Proverbs 11:25) When you live for others, you live forever—because you out-live your generation by the legacy you live behind after you depart into glory to be with the Lord. But when you live to yourself, when you are reduced to SELF—you are easily forgotten when you die and depart in glory.

Permit me to admonish you today to live your life to be a blessing to a soul connected to you today. I want you to know that so many souls are connected and looking up to you, and through you so many souls will be saved and rescued from destruction. Will you disciple someone today to find Jesus Christ?

As a genuine Christian; it is your duty to evangelize Jesus Christ to all you meet on your way. Jesus is still in the healing business— Jesus is still doing miracles from time of old to now. Therefore, tell someone about Jesus Christ today, disciple and bring them to Church. *Philip findeth Nathanael...* (John 1:45)

Please to prove the sincerity of your love for God today; please become a soul winner. The dignity of your Christianity is hidden in your boldness to proclaim and evangelize Jesus Christ to all you meet on your way. There is a question mark on the integrity of your Christianity until you become a life soul winner. Invite someone to join us worship the Lord Jesus this coming Sunday. Amen.

# MIRACLE OF GOD MINISTRIES

## PILLARS OF THE COMMISSION

### We Believe Preach and Practice the following:

1) We believe and preach Salvation to every living human being

2) We believe and preach Repentance and forgiveness of sins

3) We believe and preach the baptism of the Holy Spirit and Spiritual gifts

4) We believe and teach the Prosperity

5) We believe and preach Divine Healing and Miracles (Signs &Wonder)

6) We believe and preach Faith

7) We believe and proclaim the Power of God (Supernatural)

8) We believe and proclaim Praise& Worship to God

9) We believe and preach Wisdom

10) We believe and preach Holiness (Consecration)

11) We believe and preach Vision

12) We believe and teach the Word of God

13) We believe and teach Success

14) We believe and practice Prayer

15) We believe and teach Deliverance

**These 15 stones form the Pillars of Our Commission.** Become part of this church family and follow this great move of God.

# MY HEART FELT PRAYER FOR YOU

I desire to hear your testimony. I will love for you to write me as soon as you can 33 Schley street Newark New Jersey 07112. A few of my other books will also be a big blessing into your life. I will encourage you to explore some of my other books.

## Now let me Pray for you:

*O Lord God that heareth prayer, unto thee shall all flesh come. Lord Jesus, restore this precious soul that is reading this destiny restoration pillars. May their lives, career, and destiny accelerate like never before. May you grant them their heart desires and make all their plans to succeed. Give them a testimony that will forever give them reason to praise and glorify your Holy Name. Amen*

## \*\*\*\*DO NOT FORGET YOUR GOD\*\*\*\*

**"Then beware lest thou forget the Lord, which brought thee forth out of the land of Egypt, from the house of bondage." Deut 6:12**

In my own opinion knowing God is a personal thing. We are instructed to "....work out your own salvation with fear and trembling. For it is God which worketh in you both to will and to do of his good pleasure." (Phil 2:12-13)

It is my vision to see you experience a personal encounter with our Lord Jesus Christ. A lot of church folks have indirectly denied him, but I tell you the truth as long as you embrace him invisibly, He will do great things in your life.  We must always practice the ritual of daily devotion and prayer as a lifestyle. You can join our prayer-line 515-739-1216-code 162288 every Mondays, Wednesday, and Saturdays eastern time. More also you can come worship with us together at our worship center 343 Sanford avenue Newark New Jersey 07106.

Always remember God is spirit, therefore we must worship him in spirit and in truth. God is not a man that he should lie, nor the son of man that he should repent.

~Learn to honor the presence of God in your life. ~Embrace the acts and hand of God in your life. ~Respect and reverence God in your life time. ~Help spread the gospel of Jesus by winning soul for the Kingdom of God.

Finally I must talk to you about eternity! Heaven is real and we all must make conscious plan to make it at last. I hate to tell you more about hell but we must repent of our sins forsake our sins confess Jesus as Lord and embrace the gift of Salvation for us to make heaven. We must live a righteous life, worthy of emulation for others to copy for the Kingdom of God.

# ETERNITY IS REAL

It will profit us nothing as a ministry if you finish reading this book without making plans for heaven. You must make conscious plans to make heaven because eternity is real.

Indeed we live in an immoral time, sin has gained grounds and promotion that even the righteous are tempted to fall short of the glory of God.

**You might ask me, what must I do to be saved?**

As long as we believe and repent God is willing to forgive and to restore our lives "And they said, Believe on the Lord Jesus Christ, and thou shalt be saved, and thy house. (Acts 16:31)

Salvation is possible only through the name of our Lord Jesus Christ. Neither is there salvation in any other: for there is none other name under heaven given among men, whereby we must be saved. (Acts 4:12)

I admonish you therefore to think twice before you commit those sins that not only easily beset you but also separates you far away from God. As long as you repent even now, God is more than willing to restore and save your life from eternal hell fire. **And make straight paths for your feet, lest that which is lame be turned out of the way; but let it rather be healed. Follow peace with all men, and holiness, without which no man shall see the Lord: Hebrew 12:13-14**

Make conscious plans to make heaven. Change the way you approach things and God will restore and forgive you of all your sins. Amen.

# CHAPTER 4

## ABOUT THE AUTHOR

Rev Franklin N Abazie is the founding and Presiding Pastor of Miracle of God Ministries with headquarters in Newark, New Jersey USA and a branch church in Owerri- Imo State Nigeria. He is following the footsteps of one of his mentors, Oral Roberts (Healing Evangelist) of the blessed memory. The Lord passed Oral Roberts healing mantle two days before he went to be with the Lord at age 91 into the hand of healing evangelist-Rev Franklin N Abazie in a vision.

In all his services the Power and Presence of God is present to heal all in his audience. He is an ordained man of God with a Healing Ministry reviving the healing and miracle ministry of Jesus Christ of Nazareth.

Pastor Franklin N Abazie, is called by God with a unique mandate: **"THE MOMENT IS DUE TO IMPACT YOUR WORLD THROUGH THE REVIVAL OF THE HEALING & MIRACLE MINISTRY OF JESUS CHRIST OF NAZARETH "I AM SENDING YOU TO RESTORE HEALTH UNTO THEE AND I**

## WILL HEAL THEE OF THY WOUNDS. SAID THE LORD OF HOST"

Rev. Abazie is a gifted ardent Teacher of the word of God who operates also in the office of a Prophet, generating and attracting undeniable signs & wonders, special miracles and healings, with apostolic fireworks of the Holy Ghost. He is the founding and presiding senior Pastor of this fast growing Healing ministry. He has written over 86 inspirational, healing and transforming books covering almost all aspect of divine healing and life. He is happily married and blessed with children.

# BOOKS BY REV FRANKLIN N ABAZIE

*1) The Outcome of Faith*
*2) Understanding the secret of prevailing Prayers*
*3) Commanding Abundance*
*4) Understanding the secret of the man God uses*
*5) Activating my due Season*
*6) Overcoming Divine Verdicts*
*7) The Outcome of Divine Wisdom*
*8) Understanding God's Restoration Mandate*
*9) Walking in the Victory and Authority of the truth*
*10) Gods Covenant Exemption*
*11) Destiny Restoration Pillars*
*12) Provoking Acceptable Praise*
*13) Understanding Divine Judgment*
*14) Activating Angelic Re-enforcement*
*15) Provoking Un-Merited Favor*
*16) The Benefits of the Speaking faith*
*17) Understanding Divine Arrangement*
*18) Put your faith to work*
*19) Developing a positive attitude in life*
*20) The Power of Prevailing faith*
*21) Inexplicable faith*
*22) The intellectual components of Redemption.*
*23) Dominating Controlling Spirit*
*24) Understanding Divine Prosperity*
*25) Understanding the secret of the man God Uses*
*26) Retaining Your Inheritance*
*27) Never give up hope*
*28) Commanding Angelic Escorts*
*29) The winner's faith*
*30) Understanding Your Guardian Angels*
*31) Overcoming the Dominion of Sin*
*32) Understanding the Voice of God*

33) The Outstanding benefits of the Anointing
34) The Audacity of the Blood of Jesus
35) Walking in the Reality of the Anointing
36) The Mystery of Divine supply
37) Understanding Your Harvest Season
38) Activating Your Success Buttons
39) Overcoming the forces of Darkness
40) Overcoming the devices of the devil
41) Overcoming Demonic agents
42) Overcoming the sorrows of failure
43) Rejecting the Sorrows of failure
44) Resisting the Sorrows of Poverty
45) The Restoring broken Marriages.
46) Redeeming Your Days
47) The force of Vision
48) Overcoming the forces of ignorance
49) Understanding the sacrifice of small beginning
50) The might of small beginning
51) Praying in the Spirit
52) Dominating controlling Spirits
53) Breaking the shackles of the curse of the law
54) Covenant keys to answered prayers
55) Wisdom for Signs & Wonders
56) Wisdom for generational Impact
57) Wisdom for Marriage Stability
58) Understanding the number of your Days
59) Enforcing Your Kingdom Rights
60) Escaping the traps of immoralities
61) Escaping the trap of Poverty
62) Accessing Biblical Prosperity
63) Accessing True Riches in Christ
64) Silencing the Voice of the Accuser
65) Overcoming the forces of oppositions
66) Quenching the voice of the avenger
67) Silencing demonic Prediction & Projection
68) Silencing Your Mocker

# MIRACLE OF GOD MINISTRIES

*NIGERIA CRUSADE*
*2012*

**MIRACLE OF GOD
MINISTRIES**

*NIGERIA CRUSADE
2012*

## MIRACLE OF GOD
## MINISTRIES

*NIGERIA CRUSADE*
*2012*

CPSIA information can be obtained
at www.ICGtesting.com
Printed in the USA
LVHW030030271122
733857LV00007B/717

9 781945 133497